LOOK OUT!

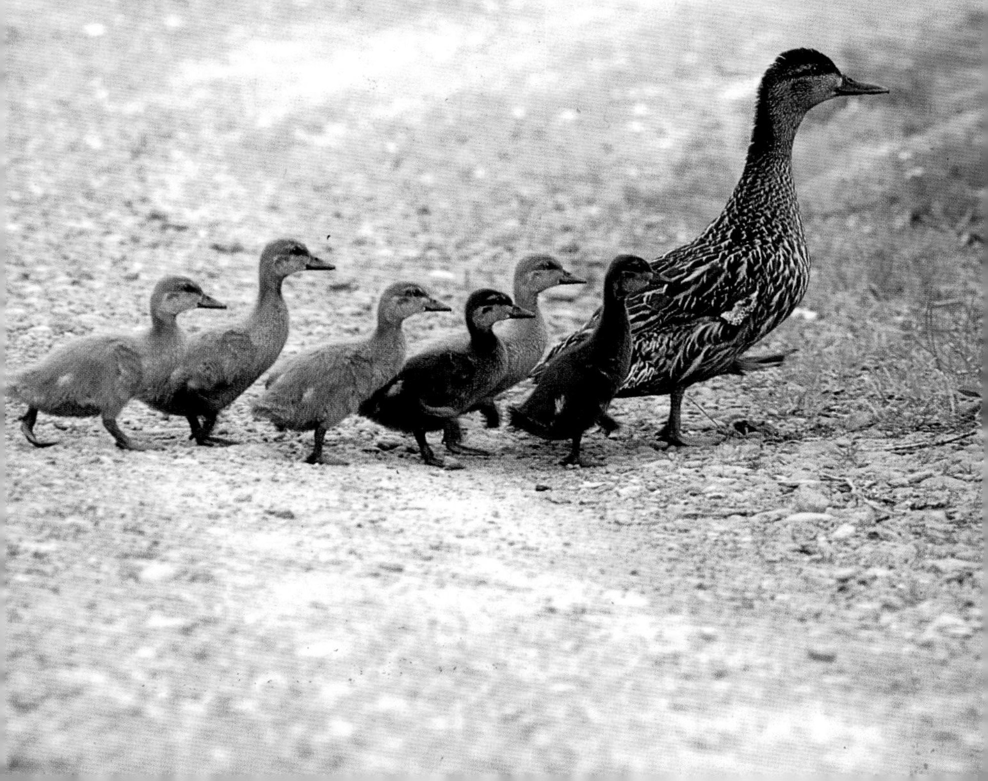

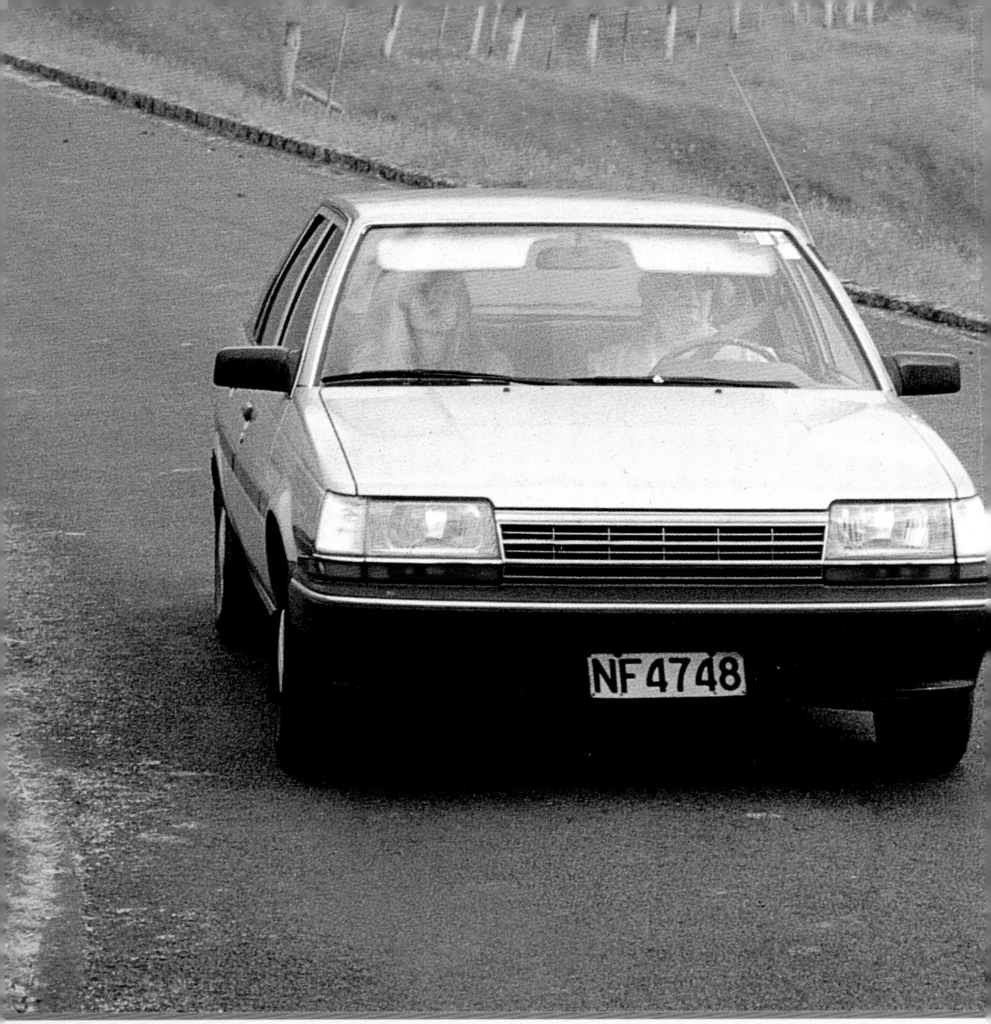
NF 4748

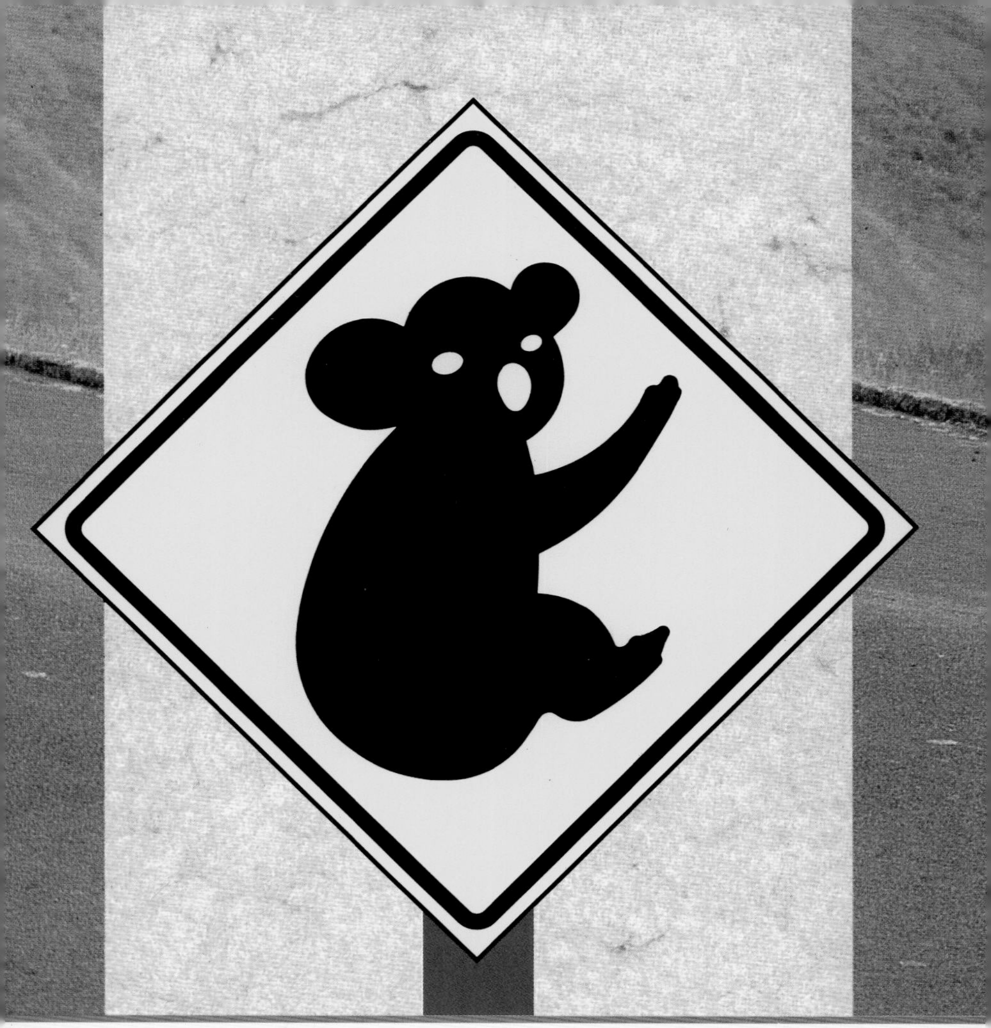

Look out!

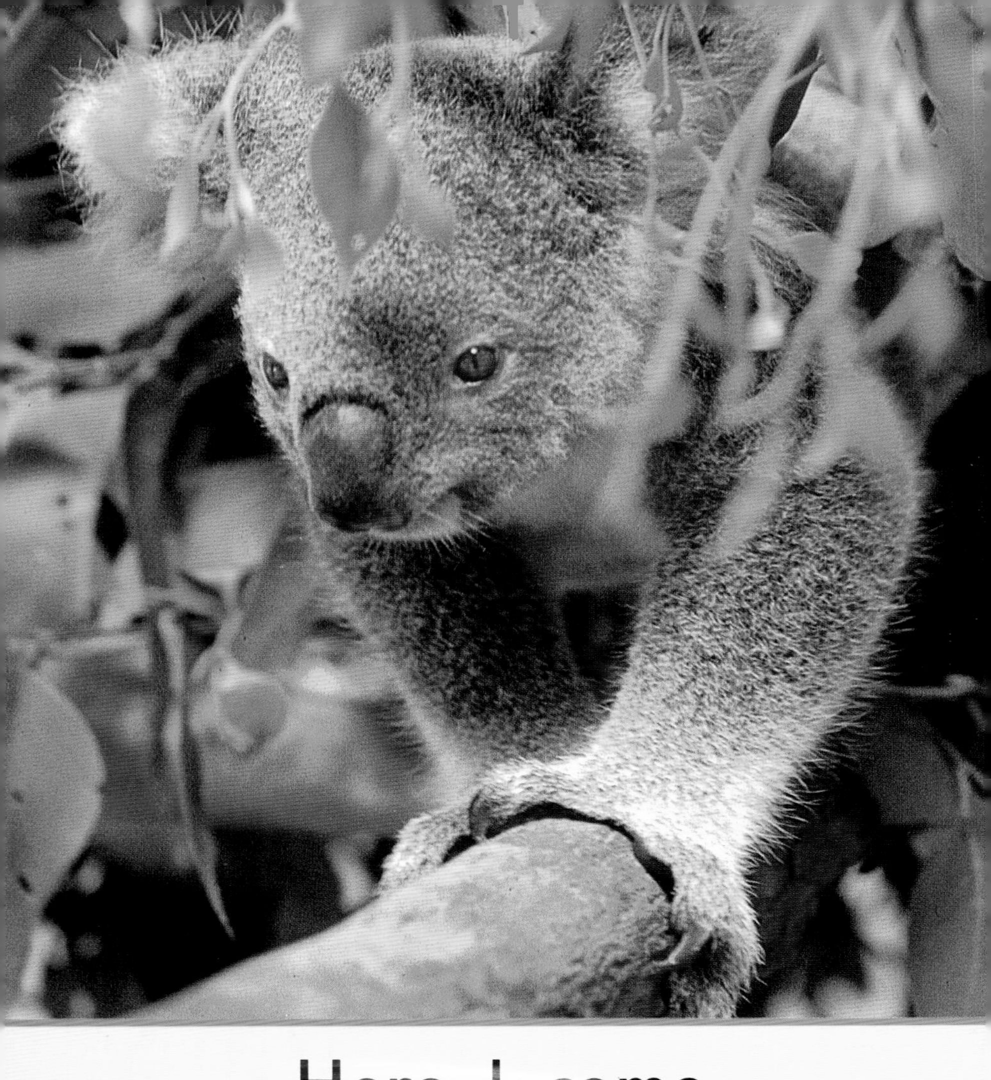

Here I come.

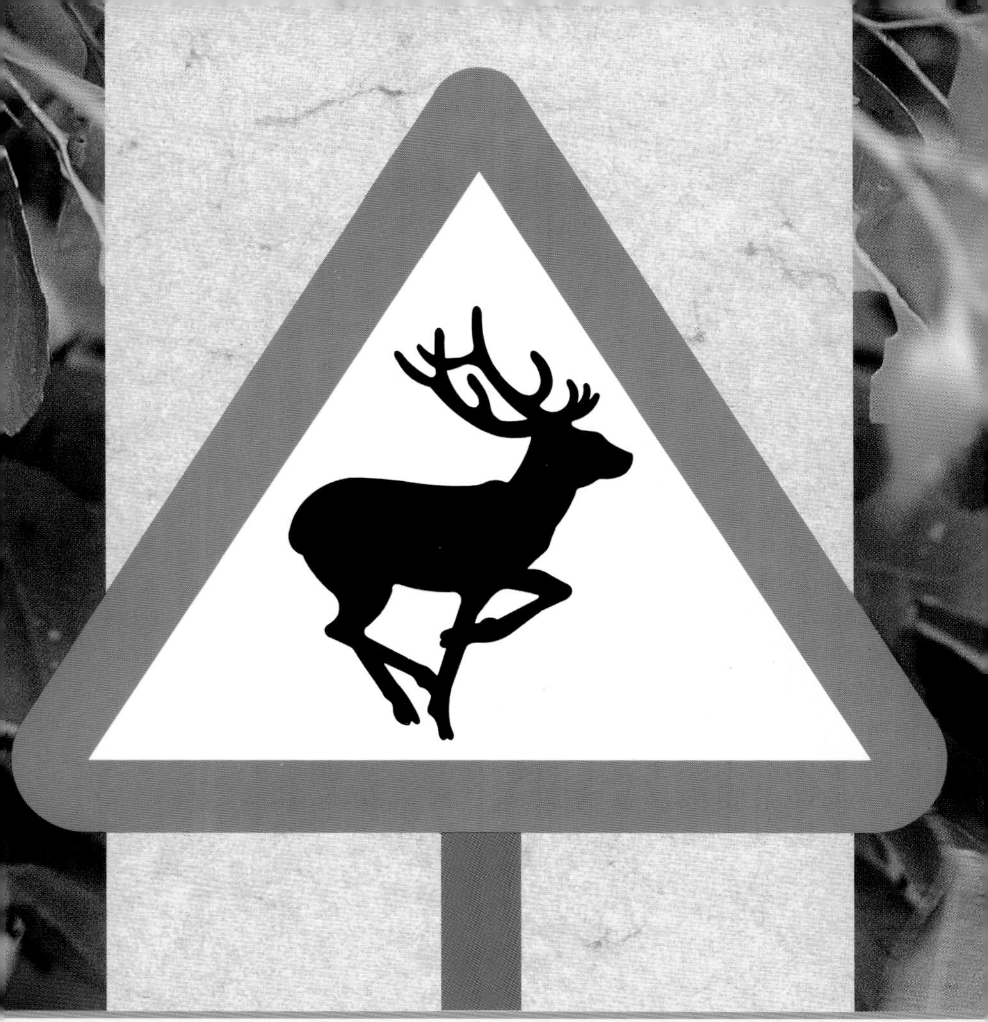

Look out!

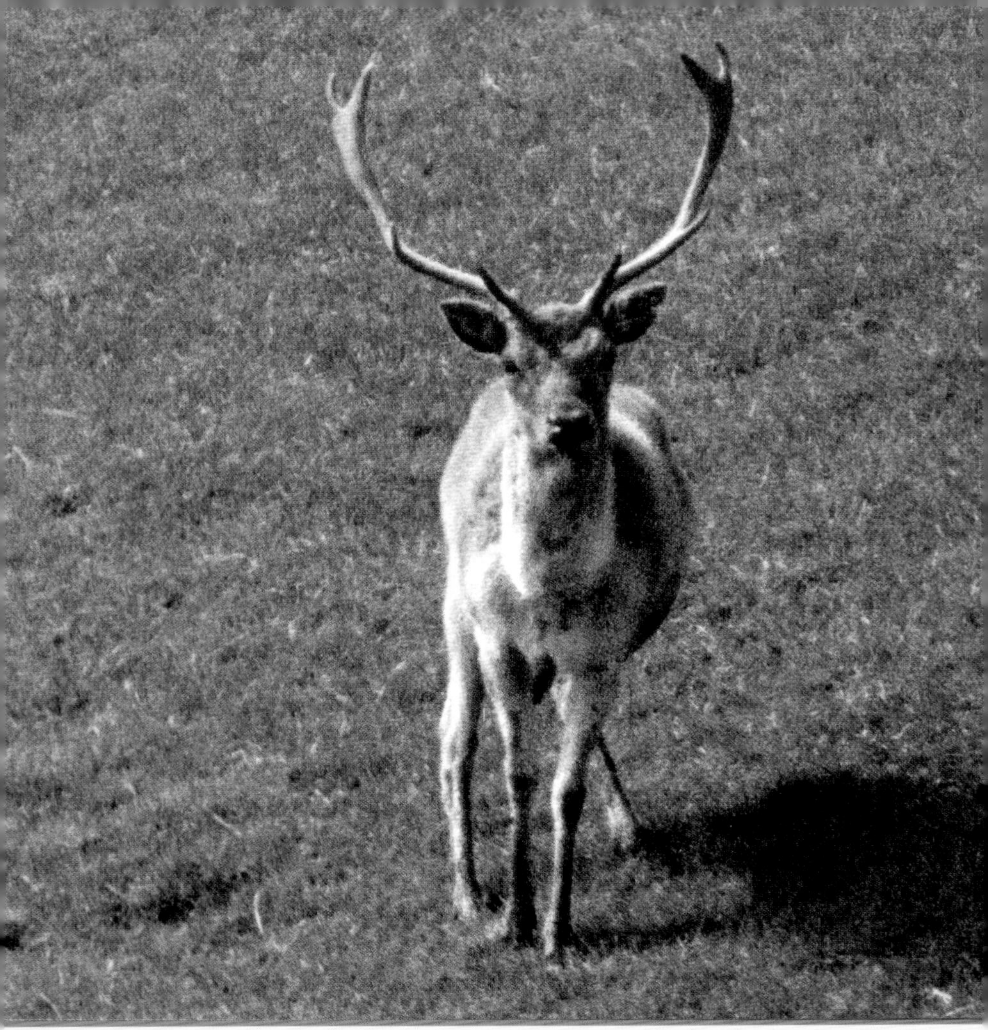

Here I come.

Look out!

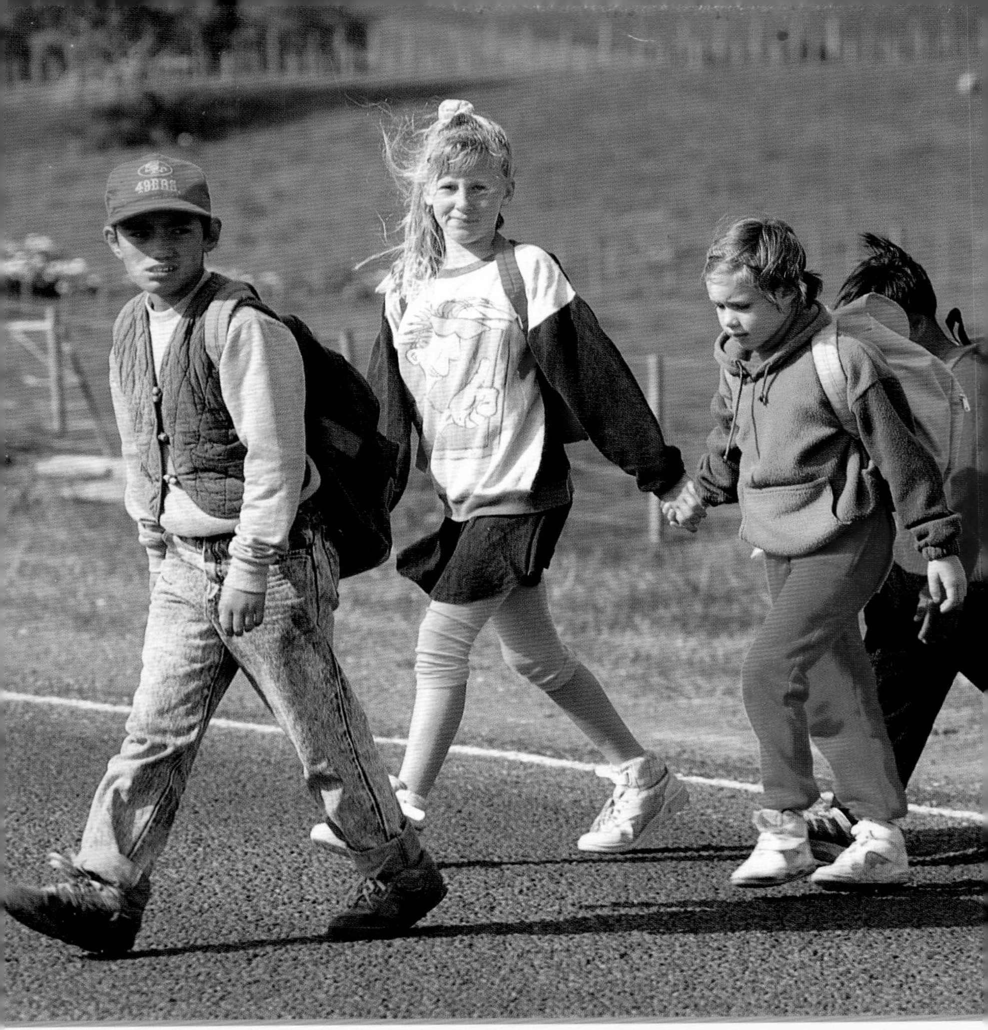

Here we come.